Your
Jewish
Child

YOUR JEWISH CHILD

MORRISON DAVID BIAL

Illustrated by LEN EPSTEIN

UNION OF
AMERICAN HEBREW CONGREGATIONS

My most heartfelt thanks to Rabbi Daniel Syme
who was guide, goad, and friend
in the final stages of the manuscript of this book

To the members of Temple Sinai,
Summit, New Jersey,
who have just celebrated
the Temple's silver anniversary
as I embark on my silver anniversary
as Rabbi of Temple Sinai

THE FELDMAN LIBRARY FUND was created in 1974 through a gift from the Milton and Sally Feldman Foundation. THE FELDMAN LIBRARY FUND, which provides for the publication by the UAHC of selected outstanding Jewish books and texts, memorializes Sally Feldman who in her lifetime devoted herself to Jewish youth and Jewish learning. Herself an orphan and brought up in an orphanage, she dedicated her efforts to helping Jewish young people get the educational opportunities she had not enjoyed.

In loving memory of my beloved wife Sally
"She was my life, and she is gone,
She was my riches, and I am a pauper."

"Many daughters have done valiantly,
but thou excellest them all."

MILTON E. FELDMAN

Contents

Editor's Introduction

In May of 1976, a revealing survey appeared in the UAHC's educational publication *Compass*. Entitled "Teach Us What We Want to Teach," the study asked parents what questions they would most like to be able to answer for their children. Surprisingly, a great majority of the most desired information fell under the general heading of "Basic Judaism."

This handbook for Jewish parents constitutes a beginning primer for parents or parents-to-be in many key areas of Jewish concern. Rabbi Morrison Bial has treated such topics as baby naming, prayer, God, death, holidays, and simple ritual in an engaging and interesting manner.

High school and college students will also find this book of great value in approaching and understanding basic Jewish teachings and values. We hope that this book will be an important first step in a lifetime of Jewish study and experience.

Many individuals contributed their special talents to the production of *Your Jewish Child*. Rabbi Steven M. Reuben and Rabbi Leonard A. Schoolman read the manuscript and made many helpful suggestions. Ralph Davis, UAHC Director of Publications, and his talented staff transformed the typed manuscript into the lovely volume you have before you.

We hope that you enjoy *Your Jewish Child* and that it will help to make your home a true center of Jewish learning and identity in years to come.

Rabbi Daniel B. Syme

Introduction

You're expecting a baby or you have just had one. *Mazal tov!* Undoubtedly you've begun to think about the tremendous responsibility ahead—that of shaping a human life.

As Jewish parents, you've also probably discussed the question of how to create a *Jewish* home for your child. That's what this book is all about.

Whether or not your own Jewish education was an intense one, this book will help you teach your child. And we think that you will enjoy learning as well.

We start with the premise that you want your baby to grow to be a Jew, a thinking, aware, secure, and informed Jew. This is an important goal.

Being a Jew

As a Jew you are part of one of the oldest religious systems in the world. Whether you were born a Jew or have been converted to Judaism, you belong to a religion and a people that has given the world much of its spiritual, ethical, and cultural heritage. You are part of a religion and people that is four thousand years old.

Our Judaism demands a high ethical standard, a regard for all humanity, and the need to bring respect and understanding to all human relationships.

Judaism links us with our people, the Jewish people, throughout the world. It links us with our brothers and sisters in Israel and the development of our old-new land. It conveys a sense of the creativity and concern that have been characteristic of Judaism ever since we became a people and a religion.

Judaism also directs us in our relationship with God, a relationship that requires no intermediaries, no superstitions. Judaism calls for the best that is within us, the development of character, the fulfillment of our natural abilities, and the creative growth of our personalities.

That's Where You Come In

No one is closer to a child than his or her parents. The child who grows with a feeling of love, of being wanted, of having a place in the family and in God's world will almost certainly grow to be a strong mature person. The child whose emotional and spiritual needs are not provided for often will not.

This book is meant as a guide to young Jewish parents, to help you and your spouse build a Jewish home as a positive and responsive center of your lives. We believe that you will find such a home to be a most rewarding aspect of your marriage and parenthood. There is little to lose except a bit of time, but there is a whole world to gain.

Rabbis tell this ancient story: When God was ready to give the Torah to Israel, He asked the people assembled at Mount Sinai: "What guarantee will you give Me for My Torah?" The people answered: "The patriarchs, Abraham, Isaac, and Jacob, will be our guarantee." God said: "The patriarchs had their faults." The people then said: "Let the prophets be our guarantee." God said: "The prophets, too, have their faults." The Israelites said: "Let our children be our guarantee." God responded: "They are the best guarantee. I will accept your children" (Shir Hashirim Rabbah).

Our children are our hope and our legacy to the future. So let's take a look at how your children's Jewish education can begin.

Your
Jewish
Child

1.

YOU AND YOUR CHILD

How Important Is the Home?

Your home will be the single most important
influence in the Jewish upbringing and fundamental
Jewish education of your child. From earliest times,
Judaism has been based on the supposition that the
home is the foundation of our religion. This is sound
psychology, for many researchers hold that fundamental
attitudes and values are established before the age of six.
By school age, the child has already made major strides
in physical and mental growth and, when prepared

correctly, in spiritual growth as well. Being sent to religious school to get first impressions of Judaism at the age of five or six is far better than at eight or nine; yet, it is evident that even at five or six, religion will no longer be accepted quite as naturally as walking, talking, or responding to parental affection. Religion is accepted as a natural part of life when it begins as soon as children are aware of life and the world around them.

You should really discuss the religious rearing of your children *before* the children are born. There are some basic questions which you should carefully consider.

Shouldn't We Give Our Children Freedom of Choice?

Shouldn't we practice democracy in religion as we do in politics? Shouldn't we wait until our children are old enough to make up their own minds as to whether they want to learn about religion or be religious? Isn't imposing our religion on our children unfair?

Actually, waiting until the child is sufficiently mature to decide such a question is self-defeating. Surely you won't wait to teach your child to read or write, to learn a musical instrument, to swim or play ball until that learning is motivated by conscious decision-making. Waiting destroys the chance to master a skill as if it were inborn. Only the unusual individual overcomes a late start. This is equally true with the ethical convictions, moral foundations, and practical skills of religion.

It is through the parent-child relationship that the child's religious values and attitudes are shaped and developed. Your youngster will identify with you and initially adopt your attitudes, your values, your customs, and your vision of life. Parents, consciously or unconsciously, teach lessons explicitly stated and implicitly contained in their own approach to life, in their own philosophy, in their own sense of being.

So don't wait. Your reluctance to teach is a lesson in itself. Your wish to have a Jewish home and Jewish children is the lesson your children need.

Can't We Depend on the Religious School?

The religious school has an important role to play, yet it is secondary to religious instruction in the home. As your children mature, their world will expand to include the synagogue and religious school, the neighborhood and the community. In this enlarged "universe" children will flourish if their roots have been developed within a Jewish home.

The child who must wait for religious school instruction for his or her first real taste of Judaism may learn to feel secure as a Jew. The intellect may absorb the lessons. But the joy and ease of religion that come from early absorption in the most favorable place of growth, the home, may not appear as we hope they will.

The religious school provides education in a synagogal setting, teaching the *facts* and *skills* of holidays, Hebrew, worship, and a variety of other content areas. Its role, at best, is complementary to that of the home.

Primary teaching at home makes it possible for religious school instruction to have a life of its own, rather than being something plastered on to public school instruction. Ideally, religious school is a widening and deepening of that which was implanted in the years of childhood.

The importance of this early preschool training is underlined by the discouraging reports of some religious schools in their endeavors to create mature and dedicated Jews. Such reports of difficulty, by the way, are shared by non-Jewish religious educators as well. Indeed, the uncaring home can *undo* the work of the best religious school. The best teaching is of little effect if the constant response at home is indifference. If *you* prepare your children for religious training, and if they feel your personal commitment, then religious school will reinforce home life. That's what we're after.

How Much Should We Know?

There are any number of ways to increase your own Jewish knowledge. Every synagogue offers courses. There are correspondence courses through the UAHC for those who have no school near their homes. And, of course, independent reading of Jewish books can be of immense value. In preparing to help your children, you will also add to your own knowledge and appreciation of Judaism.

There are dozens of worthwhile publications touching on every possible content area and interpretation of Judaism. You will find a selected, annotated bibliography in the last pages of this volume, and your first action after reading this work might be to begin to read, study, and discuss.

There is great value in learning how to *read* Hebrew. A knowledge of *spoken* Hebrew is enjoyable as well, yet it is more difficult to master and not necessary for everyday Jewish life. In learning to *read* Hebrew you'll have plenty of help. This book, for example, supplies all the Hebrew in transliteration. Even the new *Shaarei Tefillah, Gates of Prayer*, the official Reform Jewish prayer book, offers much of its Hebrew transliterated in a special section. Perhaps your accent will not sound fresh from Jerusalem, but you can most certainly have the satisfaction of singing and praying in Hebrew.

The history and ideas of Judaism and the Jewish people form a great body of material, but even the study of one or two books can mean the difference between recognition and ignorance. The great Jewish teacher, Hillel, in ending his formulation of the Golden Rule, said: "That is the whole Torah; the rest is but commentary. Now, go and learn!" We, too, must "go and learn."

Should We Consider a Jewish Nursery School?

A Jewish nursery school can be most valuable. If one is available, by all means enroll your children. The young pupils of such a school usually learn very well and happily what it is to be a Jew. The Jewish nursery school has proved its worth to many parents and children. Wherever possible, of course, the Jewish nursery school selected should be consistent with the religious orientation of your home.

2.

JEWISH ELEMENTS OF YOUR HOME

The Mezuzah

There are certain objects which will give your home a distinctive Jewish character.

A *mezuzah* is obviously the first item to mention, for it greets us as we enter a Jewish home. The *mezuzah* should be affixed to the entrance doorpost at eye height at the right as we enter. It is set at an angle, the top tilted inward. The case is made of metal, stoneware, wood, or other material and is inscribed with either the word *Shaddai*, a name for God, or just the letter *shin*, the first letter of that word. There is often an opening in the case through which the word, written on the enclosed parchment, is visible. *Shaddai* is not only God's name. It also stands for the Hebrew words *Shomer daltot Yisrael*, "Guardian of the doors of Israel."

The case is hollow and contains a tiny scroll of parchment on which the *Shema*, "Hear O Israel," and two paragraphs from Deuteronomy (6:4-9 and 11:13-21) are hand printed. The *mezuzah* fulfills the biblical injunction contained in the *Veahavta*: "You shall write them on the doorposts of your houses. . . ."

The *mezuzah* is an unmistakable sign of a Jewish home. The rabbis taught that the moral purpose of the *mezuzah* is to teach that all our possessions are the gift of God. Traditional Jews touch the case as they pass and then kiss their fingers as a sign of their love of God and their gratitude for His protection. In addition, they affix a *mezuzah* to the doorpost of *every* room of their home (excluding the bathroom and the storeroom). Most liberal Jews affix a *mezuzah* only at each entrance of the home.

Affixing a Mezuzah

When you move into a new home, the fixing of the *mezuzah* should be a family ceremony. Any Jew may conduct the brief ritual. The blessing you recite before nailing or screwing the *mezuzah* onto the doorposts is:

Baruch Atah Adonai, Eloheinu Melech haolam, asher kideshanu bemitzvotav, vitzivanu likboa mezuzah.

"Blessed are You, O Lord our God, Ruler of the

universe, who has sanctified us through His mitzvot and commanded us to affix a *mezuzah*."

We conclude by joining together in the blessing we recite at all happy occasions:

Baruch Atah Adonai, Eloheinu Melech haolam, shehecheyanu, vekiyemanu, vehigiyanu lazman hazeh. "Blessed are You, O Lord our God, Ruler of the universe, who has given us life, sustained us, and permitted us to reach this happy occasion."

If a number of *mezuzot* are placed at one time, the one benediction suffices for them all. After the ceremony, have a bit of wine and cake, celebrating the opportunity to say a special blessing.

If you move into a home previously owned by a Jewish family, they may leave their *mezuzot*. You should, of course, offer to purchase them. If you sell your home to a non-Jew, the *mezuzot* should be removed when you leave. The scrolls within the *mezuzot* are considered sacred, as they bear the name of God.

Your child may take a role in the *mezuzot* ritual. Explain that the *mezuzot* are being put up as a sign of your dedicating your home to a Jewish way of life. Even a little child will understand.

Art and Decoration

A child grows surrounded by things that shape his or her emerging consciousness. Art and ceremonial objects on the walls and shelves will add to the recognition that yours is a Jewish home. There should be something of Jewish significance in your child's own room as well to emphasize his or her Jewish heritage.

Almost every synagogue has a Judaica shop or conducts art sales at which Jewish pictures and statues may be purchased. There are galleries in larger cities that feature Israeli art. A grand reason for a pilgrimage to Israel is to seek out its artistic and ceremonial creations. Modern Israeli art is often strikingly beautiful, and lithographs and serigraphs are colorful and inexpensive.

Biblical scenes and personalities, pictures of modern and ancient Israel, busts of great rabbis, scholars, and Zionists of yesterday and today, all mark the home as Jewish. They convey a tone, a graphic rendering of the Jewish spirit.

Nor should you overlook the artisan's creation of ceremonial objects. These include handsome Shabbat candlesticks; a brass, silver, or walnut Chanukah menorah; a metal or stoneware Pesach plate; a *Havdalah* spice box for the close of the Shabbat, often in the shape of a tower, pomegranate, or a fish; a silver base for the braided *Havdalah* candle; a metal or olivewood case for the Sukot *etrog;* or handworked velvet bags for *talit* and *tefilin.*

Some people collect Israeli stamps, coins, or medals. In addition to their artistic worth and value, they offer an illustrated history of the Jewish people and a hobby that your child can share.

The Library

A Jewish home without a Jewish library is a contradiction. There are books for children and adults, books for reference, books to be studied, books from which to pray, to learn, and to enjoy. For a good start towards a basic Jewish library, see the bibliography at the end of this volume.

Bibles and Prayer Books Are Special

We treat all books with respect, but Bibles, prayer books, and, most particularly, Torah scrolls possess a special worth. The rabbis taught that we may not place any of these on the ground, sit on them, or use them for ordinary purposes such as a doorstop or a sunshade. Nor, according to tradition, may any other book be placed on a Bible. A Bible may be placed on a prayer book, but not vice versa, and no other book may be placed on a prayer book.

According to *halachah*, Jewish law, if a Torah scroll falls from a person's grasp, that person and all who witness the fall must fast to the end of the day. If a printed Bible or prayer book falls, the person who drops it kisses its cover after picking it up. So too, according to tradition, if you discover a Torah scroll or Hebrew Bible owned by someone who does not respect it, you should purchase it—but not if an exorbitant price is demanded. Nor should young children be given a Torah scroll, even though it is a copy, or a Hebrew prayer book, until they are old enough to appreciate the gift and treat it with respect.

These teachings exemplify the deep regard and respect which Judaism accords to its special treasures. Though we live in a different world from that of our ancestors, we retain our reverence for the prayer book, the Bible, and the Torah.

Jewish Music

Your record player can be a significant element in teaching your child that yours is a Jewish home. Just as we want our children to hear the finest music of our classical culture, so too Jewish music, Israeli music, Yiddish folk songs, and classical music by Jewish composers should come to be valued and appreciated. Above all, the ceremonial objects, records, and Jewish books in your home should be used. It is good to purchase them and have them on display in your home. It is even more desirable to bless the candles on Shabbat and holidays, to lift the Kiddush cup in praise, to read, to study, and to pray. Your children will recognize that you and your spouse truly care for your Judaism and that it is an ongoing part of their own heritage.

3.

BEFORE CHILDREN ARRIVE

A Mandate of Judaism

The very first command of the Bible, made to
Adam and Eve, was "Be fruitful and multiply" (Genesis
1:28). To this day, traditional Jews consider this command to be directed to them and thus are very much
against so-called Family Planning or Planned Par-

enthood. They look upon every birth as a heavenly gift and a large family as a blessing.

Liberal Jews, however, may or may not use contraceptive methods as they choose. Any method that is medically sound and does not prevent further conception is fine. Operations that prohibit further conception, whether male or female, are generally discouraged until there is a family of two or more children—and for good reason.

The Jewish Birth Rate! An Alarming Trend!

Since the close of the Nazi era the Jewish birth rate has been one of the lowest in the world. Modern Jews are barely reproducing themselves, if that. Marriage later in life, particularly among professionals, a greater incidence of divorce, and more intermarriages are a few of the major contributing factors. The most important reason is the growing tendency of many couples to limit the number of children to one or two, which results in an absolute decline in Jewish births and in the number of Jews.

The outlook is not bright for the Jewish population of North America or Europe—or even Israel—as more and more Jews reflect reproductive patterns of the white, urban, middleclass, and professional groups—or rates even lower. Recently, the average annual Jewish birth rate in the United States was reported as about eight per thousand. Compare this with the worldwide average of 20 to 30 per thousand. Even in Israel, Jews have a 16.7 rate, while Palestinian Arabs have one of the highest rates in the world, approximately 40 per thousand.

At this writing, the average age of Americans is

twenty-seven. The average age of American Jews is thirty-eight. One of the strangest aspects of this problem is that Jews are prominent on the boards of groups seeking to reduce world population, even though the number of Jews in the world is barely holding its own in absolute terms and is dropping significantly in proportionate terms.

Three decades after the Holocaust there were still four million fewer Jews in the world than when Hitler began his mass murders. In those thirty years, the population of the world almost doubled, while that of the Jews diminished by 25 per cent. Population controls are needed in lands where human growth is outstripping economic or food production. But for Jews, a zero population growth may well result in the ultimate disappearance of our people. That is why many contemporary Jewish leaders are urging young couples to consider larger families.

Tay-Sachs Disease

A most serious warning. By a strange quirk, Jews of central or eastern European origin bear the genes of Tay-Sachs syndrome, a recessive lethal disease found predominantly in Jews. If there is any possibility that you or your mate is of this background, you should arrange for a genetic typing with your physician. It is important to know if you are a carrier. There is a simple blood test for Tay-Sachs carriers, and if only one or neither of you is a carrier of the gene, you can relax and not worry. As it occurs in only one of nine-hundred Jewish couples, the danger of being a carrier is not great. If both of you are carriers, you should have genetic counseling. However, this does not mean that you should give up the idea of having children together. During the first month of pregnancy, your obstetrician can examine the amniotic fluid. There is a 25 per cent chance of having an affected fetus, a 50 per cent chance that it will be a carrier, and a 25 per cent chance that it will not be a carrier. If there is no problem, the infant should be normal in every way. If the fluid proves that the fetus is affected, there could be an induced abortion. A child with Tay-Sachs disease cannot live beyond a very few years and the death is cruel for both child and parents.

Happily, even if both parents have the gene there is no reason why they should not have a large and healthy family, if they take the proper precautions.

4.

GOD AND JUDAISM

When Shall We Begin?

Even when children are very young, parents can begin to speak about God. Child psychologists have discovered that many youngsters have a capacity to ask questions about God (such as "where did everything come from?") as early as the age of three. Refinement of the idea will come with age, but this initial learning experience will help establish a firm foundation for further growth.

The earliest teachings should involve concrete experiences for your child. They should include the learning of blessings and the indication that prayers are addressed to God. A two-or three-year-old can know that these important elements of life are addressed to an unseen but felt Presence, the Source of life. Your children will acquire a notion of the presence of God in the world and in their own lives.

What Can We Teach?

The learning theory of Harvard psychologist Jerome Bruner suggests an additional value of teaching about God at an early age through concrete examples from your child's own experiences. Bruner insists that any subject may be taught to any child at any age in some intellectually honest form. Furthermore, his experiments have demonstrated that providing children with simple concrete indicators of complex concepts at an early age may facilitate their mastery of those concepts later in life.

In teaching about God, such indicators may include the orderly change of seasons, the sun coming up every day, the beauty and order of the world around us, and others. We stress again, however, that children conceptualize God in concrete terms, no matter how adults explain Him. This is normal and natural. You must provide concrete "suggestions" of God which children can understand. For the time being, the world around them is their theological training ground.

Teaching Your Children about God— Universal Questions

Your child will ask questions about God. Some youngsters will ask discerning questions right next to others that seem nonsensical. Both, however, are important to the child and must be respected. "Where was God before the world was born?" "When will God die?" "Is God a man?" "Why can't I see Him?" "Who was God's mother and father?" And so on.

Even before your child begins to ask questions, you must begin to teach simply what Judaism holds basic. It must be on the child's level and yet not be so simplified as to be untrue. It is generally not a good idea to teach something that must be unlearned later. It must be positive, so that the mind may grasp affirmative statements and then be able to build its own concept of God.

Here is a brief presentation of basic Jewish beliefs that four- or five- year-old children find in keeping with their own understanding. Even some younger children may be ready.

God Is One

There is only one God. Other religions of the past have believed in many gods. They had a sun god, a moon god, a god of nature, and many, many others. But Judaism is different. For thousands of years, we have believed that there is only one God for the entire world.

The Idea of God as Creator and Order in the World

Traditional Judaism speaks of God as the Creator of the world. Though the Torah describes a creation process of six days, we know that it really took billions of years, a process of evolution. The important lesson of the story, however, is that there is an order in the world, a basic plan, a structure which we attribute to that which we call God. The seasonal cycles, the regularity of day and night, and the wonder of the human body are all concrete examples of this order in creation.

The Idea of God as Unseen

Unseen things can be very real. If I say that I love you, my love is an unseen expression of our relationship. You can't say to me: "Take out your love and show it to me." Yet my love is real. If I have an idea and tell you about it, you can't say: "Take out your idea and show it to me." Nevertheless, the idea is "real."

God too is unseen yet is everywhere in the world. Therefore, we cannot ask what He looks like. Yet God is real, far more real than just an idea. Like love, we know God through signs and physical manifestations in our world.

The Idea of God as Father

This is the ancient Jewish way of referring to God. Tell your child that it has become customary to speak of God as "He."

The Jewish people of long ago believed that God was like a Father, watching over them, making sure that they were safe, giving them food through nature, and answering their prayers. The language that they used was passed on from one generation to the next. But God is not a man—nor a woman. We speak of Him in human

terms because this is the only means of expression that
we have.

The Torah

Reform Jews have many different beliefs about
how the Torah was created. Some think that God wrote
the Torah or dictated it to Moses on Mt. Sinai. The great
majority, however, believe that the Torah was written by
inspired human beings. These people wanted to explain
their world, to record their history, and to create a
society guided by laws and ethics. We like to think that
these Jews were inspired by God, because the things
which they wrote thousands of years ago are still important today.

We, too, have a right to elaborate the Torah for our
own times. Inspired men and women of our generation
must carry on this dynamic process of growth, as will our
children.

The Soul

Judaism teaches that each person is created in
the image of God. Thus, every human being has the
potential to act in ways which reflect a sense of godliness. This godliness within us is referred to as the soul.
It represents our capacity to see justice, compassion,
kindness, and love as godly and to express them in our
lives.

The Shema

Prayer is one of the first ways in which children begin to express a relationship with God. The *Shema* is a logical starting point. As soon as your child is old enough to say the words and to realize to some degree that it is a holy phrase, teach it. The *Shema* affirms that there is a God and He is One. It is basic Judaism.

Shema Yisrael, Adonai Eloheinu, Adonai echad.
"Hear O Israel, the Lord is our God, the Lord is One."

Parents as Models

The God concept is linked with the ideas of love and compassion. For almost all children, parents are the embodiment of these ideas. Therefore, the warmth and affection of your personal relationship will in some ways come to be associated with the love and compassion ascribed to God.

So, too, with the ideas of charity and kindness. We can tell children that God cares about the poor and suffering but, unless there exists a model for these concepts, they remain mere words. Parents must create models for young children. Praising individuals who show generosity or kindness, condemning cruel actions, positively reinforcing your child's sharing with others—all these help to generate new learning and new values.

When you plan your charitable contributions—to the synagogue or to any worthy cause—involve your children in the discussion. They should know that the Hebrew word for charity is *tsedakah. Tsedakah* comes from the Hebrew word that means "justice." In Judaism, giving to the poor or needy is not charity. It is doing that which is just and is an expression of godliness in the world.

It is not surprising that the word *mitzvah*, which originally meant only "commandment," has come to mean a good deed. God's commandment and a good deed are the same thing.

The Importance of Stories

Stories drawn from our Jewish heritage can be important teaching devices. The lives of Abraham, Jacob, Moses, Sarah, Rebeccah, and Rachel contain references to God's presence in the world without defining Him. The Union of American Hebrew Congregations has published some wonderful books about God, written especially for children. Two in particular are worthy of note:

1. *About God* by Molly Cone.

   Ten stories dealing with the questions children ask about God, richly illustrated in color. The leader's guide by Rabbi Daniel B. Syme will assist you in discussion.

2. *The God around Us: A Child's Garden of Prayer* by Mira Brichto.

   Lovely prayers for a child in Hebrew and English, a colorful book on God in the world, complete with a teaching guide prepared by the author.

In short, teaching about God involves concrete ideas, stories, prayer, and personal example, all expressed in terms that are honest and that can be readily understood by your children.

All of these elements will be crucial in establishing a basis for spiritual and ethical growth.

For a detailed approach on how to teach the idea of God to young children, we suggest *When Children Ask about God* by Harold S. Kushner (Schocken).

5.

PRAYER—JUDAISM IN WORDS

The Bridge of Prayer

Jews have always prayed. Indeed, the prayer book is one of the special treasures of Jewish life. The blessings, psalms, and prayers of thanksgiving found in our prayer book are not only means for the individual to express a sense of reverence for life, they are reservoirs of national memories as well. Prayers recall our being freed from Egyptian slavery, the persecutions of the crusades, and the worship of our ancestors at the Temple in Jerusalem. In times of hardship, the prayer book brings the promise of hope and a world made better for all who live in it.

The Child and Prayer

You can begin to teach your children to pray when they are very young. Prayer is one way for them to participate in our Jewish heritage. From simple beginnings greater understanding grows.

The best model for Jewish participation is your personal example. Your baby can hear and see you pronounce a blessing *(berachah,* in Hebrew).

While the words may be beyond comprehension, the attitude will be clear. You are performing a special and rewarding action.

There is a way that even tiny toddlers can participate. As soon as they can talk, babies can say "Amen."

Amen

The word Amen provides us with the first tool of prayer. This is an important word, used perhaps by more people in the world than any other. It is a Hebrew word meaning "it is so." From it we get the word *emunah,* the Hebrew word for faith.

Jews say Amen after every *berachah.* Traditionally, a blessing is a prayer of thanks to God that begins, "Blessed are You, O Lord our God . . . ," such as the blessing over bread, wine, or Shabbat candles. The person who says Amen on hearing another pronounce a *berachah* is

counted as though he or she said the whole blessing. As
soon as your youngsters can recognize that you are
saying a prayer, they can join in the *berachah*. The child
can say Amen and thereby fully participate in prayer as
a member of the family and as a Jew.

A Blessing for Every Meal

After the Second Temple in Jerusalem was de-
stroyed in 70 C.E., the rabbis of the Talmud said that the
tables which we ate upon would substitute for the altars
of the Temple. Thus, Jews have traditionally begun each
meal with the following *berachah*, as a sign of thanks for
life's many blessings:
*Baruch Atah Adonai, Eloheinu Melech haolam,
hamotzi lechem min haaretz.*
"Blessed are You, O Lord our God, Ruler of the
universe, who brings forth bread from the earth."
Beginning each meal with this blessing helps give
Jewish significance to every family meal. You can begin
saying blessings and Amen even before your baby begins to speak, so that the sound of Hebrew will not be
strange.
When blessings are recited often, many Jewish parents
discover that their children's first words include Hebrew.
There are other *berachot* (plural of *berachah*). They
are short, easy to learn, and connected with tangible
things. Your child can see the bread, wine, or the candles
being lit. The blessing is a form of thanksgiving that
even the smallest child can understand. *Berachot* are the
Jew's response of gratitude for God's blessings.
Our ancestors wanted to thank God for all the experi-

ences of life, both the usual and unusual. So there are traditional blessings for such things as health and happiness, for the sun and the seasons, for fresh fruits, a rainbow, the miracle of birth, on seeing a king, a scholar, or the first blossoms of spring.

On Hearing Good News

All Jews recite one blessing very often. It is called the *Shehecheyanu*.
Baruch Atah Adonai, Eloheinu Melech haolam, shehecheyanu, vikiyemanu, vehigiyanu lazman hazeh.
"Blessed are You, O Lord our God, who has kept us in life, sustained us, and brought us to this time."
This blessing is not only recited on holidays or at a Bar or Bat Mitzvah or other joyous occasions. Traditional Jews will recite it the first time they eat a fruit or vegetable that year, especially if it is a favorite food. They also say it if they hear good news of a personal nature, such as a birth, an engagement, or a wedding.

There is another blessing:
Baruch Atah Adonai, Eloheinu Melech haolam, hatov vehameitiv.
"Blessed are You, O Lord our God, Ruler of the universe, who is good and who does good."
This blessing is for important good news, such as the cessation of a war or some other news that benefits the community or humanity.

On Hearing Sad News

Baruch Atah Adonai, Eloheinu Melach haolam, dayan haemet.

"Blessed are You, O Lord our God, Ruler of the universe, the righteous Judge."

This blessing is recited when we hear of a death, the beginning of a war or a calamity, or anything that threatens life. It is also part of both the Reform and traditional funeral services.

The Use of Hebrew

Unless you are raising your child in Israel or in a Hebrew-speaking household, the sound of Hebrew will be unusual, but perhaps not as strange as you might imagine. If blessings are spoken daily, at the table and at bedtime, even a toddler will recognize them and participate and take pleasure in them. Since the Hebrew will come at times of family unity, your child will see Hebrew as a happy as well as a holy tongue.

Hebrew and Song

A simple Hebrew song such as *Shabbat Shalom* or *Hinei Mah Tov* is easy for a child to sing. If children can sing "Patticake," they can sing *Shabbat Shalom* too. If you know Hebrew, fine. If not, you may want to learn. Even if you don't, you can still share a bit of Hebrew with your child through song. A few blessings and prayers and some Israeli songs will give your children a headstart in their own Hebrew studies.

Youngsters absorb a new language readily when it is presented naturally. Hebrew blessings and songs and a simple vocabulary can help produce an early familiarity with the language of our people.

Some Interesting Traditional Observances

Traditional Judaism is a rich storehouse of rituals, practices, and observances. Reform Judaism is based on the premise that we are free to select from this storehouse the rituals and observances which are most relevant to us and incorporate them into our personal Jewish life style. It is interesting, then, to look at some of these traditional practices.

Particularly significant is the traditional notion that through prayer we create a relationship with God that extends from morning to evening.

The Miracle of Morning

The morning prayer in the traditional prayer book reads, "Every day You renew the miracle of Creation." So traditional Jews attempt to begin each morning with a sense of holiness and renewal. Upon waking, traditional Jews say:

Modeh ani lefanecha, Melech chai vekayam, shehechezarta bi nishmati bechemlah, rabah emunatecha.

"I thank you, O eternal King, because You have graciously restored my soul to me. Great is Your faithfulness."

They then rise and wash their hands. Before washing their hands they recite this benediction:

Baruch Atah Adonai, Eloheinu Melech haolam, asher kideshanu bimitzvotav, vetzivanu al netilat yadayim.

"Blessed are You, O Lord our God, Ruler of the

Universe, who sanctified us by Your laws and commanded us on washing hands."

The washing of hands upon arising in the morning is not only good hygiene. The recitation of the blessing that accompanies washing and the *Modeh Ani* prayer became yet another way that our ancestors helped to bring a sense of sanctification into the everyday act of greeting the morning.

Bedtime Prayers

When a child is put to bed, it is a time of separation at the end of a long day. If you say a few words of blessing and thanks every night even before your child is aware of their meaning, you will add a measure of security and love to their sleep and establish religious habits as well. Soon your children will be able to speak their own brief evening prayer.

Some families use the familiar words of the *Shema* as their bedtime prayer. Traditional Jews recite the *Shema* in the morning and the evening, in accordance with the biblical verse in Deuteronomy 6:7 which says: "You shall speak of them ... when you lie down and when you rise up." The idea of a brief prayer at bedtime is attractive to many. It is a way of filling your mind as you go to sleep with thoughts of blessing, thanks, and peace.

6.

SHABBAT—THE DAY OF REST

Shabbat is a day which combines rest and holiness. It is a pleasure to introduce both elements into your child's life. Practice a few lovely ceremonies in your home—Kiddush, candles, chalah, blessings, etc.—and your child will soon recognize the importance and beauty of Shabbat. Our Sabbath is so important in Jewish lore that it is one of the Ten Commandments and is often referred to as one of God's greatest gifts to the Jewish people. It brings a sense of sanctity and rest into our lives.

Your children can participate at an early age, even though synagogue attendance may be beyond their capabilities. Helping to arrange the Shabbat table, to set out the candlesticks and the wine goblets is a special role which helps mark the day as different from all others. Blowing out the match when candles are lit, sipping a drop of the Kiddush wine, or eating a piece of chalah are all means of participation for all but the youngest baby.

The chalah, the braided eggbread, may be purchased or home-baked. Orthodox Jews set out two *chalot* as a symbol of the double portion of manna eaten by our ancestors in the wilderness. We Reform Jews may use one or two.

We also use two or more candles. Some families add an extra candle for each child in addition to the usual pair. Some families invite each woman and girl to light her own two candles, but this is not usual. Candles symbolize the radiance, sanctity, and blessings of the Shabbat.

We may use wine glasses or silver goblets. You may use one wine glass or goblet for the Kiddush, passing it to other members of the family for each to take a sip; or you may give each person his or her own glass with a small portion of wine.

Welcoming the Shabbat

Before Shabbat begins, many Jews drop coins in a charity box of the Jewish National Fund. This custom arose because traditional Jews do not carry money on the Shabbat. So they combined emptying their pockets with the tradition of *tsedakah*, charity. Your child will soon learn that *tsedakah* always accompanies a happy day or event.

Prayers of Shabbat

How to begin? The Shabbat is ushered in with the lighting of candles, followed by a *berachah*. Traditionally, all blessings are said *before* performing an act. The only exception is the lighting of Shabbat candles. This is for the simple reason that, after the blessing is said, the Shabbat has arrived. Traditional Jews are forbidden to light fires on Shabbat, so one couldn't light the candles if you said the blessing first.

The candles are traditionally lit twenty minutes before sundown, but in liberal households the candles are usually lit and the blessings pronounced just before dinner the year round. This means that your little children can participate in the welcoming of Shabbat even in June, when otherwise they might be asleep. The candles are usually white, but any color may be used. The blessing is chanted or spoken.

Though any member of the family may do so, the mother customarily lights the candles and then recites the following blessing:

Baruch Atah Adonai, Eloheinu Melech haolam, asher kideshanu bemitzvotav vetzivanu lehadlik ner shel Shabbat.

"Blessed is the Lord our God, Ruler of the universe, who hallows us with His mitzvot and commands us to kindle the lights of Shabbat."

In many families, everyone joins in.

The Shabbat has now officially begun. It is traditionally the father's role to lift a cup of wine and recite the Kiddush, or sanctification of the wine, as follows:

Baruch Atah Adonai, Eloheinu Melech haolam, borei peri hagafen.

"Blessed is the Lord our God, Ruler of the universe, Creator of the fruit of the vine."

You will find the words to the Kiddush in every Shabbat prayer book. The *CCAR Shabbat Manual* contains the music and a transliteration as well. In some families, only the father sings and the others join in by saying Amen. Some families prefer to have everyone sing along. Your child will soon join in if the whole family sings together.

Blessing the Children

It has long been the custom for Jewish parents to bless their children after the Kiddush. You may place your hand on their heads or shoulders or just hold their hands.

For a boy:

Yesimcha Elohim ke-Efrayim vechi-M'nasheh.

"May God bless you as He did the sons of Joseph in ancient days."

For a girl:

Yesimech Elohim ke-Sarah, Rivka, Leah, ve-Rachel.

"May God bless you as He did Sarah, Rebecca, Leah, and Rachel."

Some people conclude with the ancient blessing:
Yevarechecha Adonai veyishmerecha.
Ya'er Adonai panav elecha vichuneka.
Yisa Adonai panav elecha, veyasem lecha shalom.
"May the Lord bless you and guard you.
May the Lord's face be bright upon you and may He be gracious to you.
May the Lord lift up His face to you and bless you with peace."
Some Liberal Jews suggest that children respond by saying:
"May God bless our parents and all our family."
Even an infant will sense the special moment of blessing.
We then either cut or break the chalah and speak or chant:
Baruch Atah Adonai, Eloheinu Melech Haolam, hamotzi lechem min haaretz.
"Blessed are You, O Lord our God, Ruler of the Universe, who brings forth bread from the earth."

The meal should be the nicest and most enjoyable of the week. The rabbis used to prepare for the Shabbat meal by purchasing the best food the marketplace could provide and their purse could afford. They said that Shabbat food tasted particularly good as there was a rare added spice. Its name? Shabbat.

Grace after the Meal

There is a long and beautiful traditional grace after the meal. There is also a much shortened Reform

version. You will find them both in the *Shabbat Manual*
(CCAR). It is also customary to prolong the Shabbat meal
by singing Hebrew songs. After the meal, of course, you
should attend temple services as a family.

The Shabbat Day

Make the Shabbat a special day for your family.
When your child is still too young for services, family
visits, museum or park going, anything that enhances life
is in accord with our concept of Shabbat. The rabbis
said: God gave each Jew an extra soul on Shabbat to be
able to contain the spiritual joy of our seventh day.

7.

THE JEWISH YEAR

The High Holy Days

The quality and character of the High Holy Days differ from all other holidays in the Jewish year. The ten days beginning with Rosh Hashanah (the Jewish New Year) and concluding with Yom Kippur (the Day of Atonement) are known as the Days of Awe. The High Holy Days fall in September or October, varying from year to year as a result of Judaism's lunar calendar.

These two holy days are not connected with a particular historical event in the life of the Jewish people, as are

most other holidays. In a very basic sense, the High Holy
Days are the most personal of all the holidays. It is a time
when we must, individually, search our inner beings,
reevaluate our life styles, reconsider our values and our
relationships with others.

Rosh Hashanah

Rosh Hashanah begins on the new moon of the
Hebrew month of Tishrei. Traditional Jews celebrate
two days of the holiday, while most Reform Jews observe only one. Rosh Hashanah is a time of family and
community celebration. We go to the synagogue, to re-
affirm with other Jews our commitment to the ethical
values of the Jewish people. Most congregations have
family or children's services as well, so that even small
children can share the importance and drama of the High
Holy Days with their family and community. One of the
most moving moments of the Rosh Hashanah service is
the blowing of the shofar. The shofar calls remind us that
the ten days between Rosh Hashanah and Yom Kippur
are to be a time of serious introspection.

The shofar also reminds us of the provocative biblical
story, read each Rosh Hashanah, of Abraham binding his
son Isaac and almost offering him as a sacrifice to God.
The shofar is symbolic of the ram, caught nearby in a
bush by its horns, which Abraham eventually substi-
tuted for Isaac as the sacrifice. We are thus reminded of
Abraham's willingness to obey God and of the break
from human sacrifice symbolized by this story.

Rosh Hashanah in the home should be a time of joy
and thankfulness. The new year is ushered in with the
lighting of holiday candles. The first course at dinner is

often sliced apples dipped in honey, as a sweet beginning to what we hope will be a sweet year. A special round chalah may be part of the home celebration as well. Contributing to a worthy cause is another positive way to usher in a year filled with hope for all people.

Yom Kippur

Yom Kippur is a time when we ask forgiveness for sins against God and our fellow human beings. The observance is centered in the synagogue, with solemn services on Kol Nidre night and throughout the day of Yom Kippur itself. Again, most synagogues have family services as well. It is a traditional time of fasting and introspection. On Yom Kippur, we are given another opportunity to examine our lives and measure them against the values taught by Judaism. We take time with our family and friends to reflect upon the quality of our relationships over the past year and resolve to renew our efforts to create peace, fairness, and love in our lives.

Home observance of Yom Kippur centers on the fast associated with this most holy day in the Jewish year. The deeper significance of fasting may be beyond the comprehension of young children, yet your child can understand that Yom Kippur is a special day set aside from all others.

Yom Kippur concludes with a break-fast. This should be a family affair, a time of togetherness and joy, a time of hope and confidence in a meaningful year-to-come.

The synagogue service, day of fasting and prayer, and culminating break-fast all help teach children that Yom Kippur is an important day set aside for looking at how we live and how we might make ourselves better human beings.

Sukot

Sukot is the biblical Jewish festival of Thanksgiving. The word *sukot* refers to the thatched, flimsy huts which symbolize the rapidly built shelters required by the desert wanderings of our ancestors. Judaism also teaches us that the sukah, the small hut, reminds the comfortable, secure Jew of the misfortunes of those in want.

Sukot is observed for eight days in traditional homes, while Reform and Israeli Jews celebrate for seven. There are temple services for the family during which the traditional symbols of the holiday, the *lulav* (combination of palm branch, willow, and myrtle) and *etrog* (citron), are waved in all directions to indicate the presence of God throughout the world.

Sukot was traditionally observed in the home where each family built its own sukah or booth. Families would then spend some time each day of the festival in the sukah, usually during meals, to fulfill the traditional commandment to "dwell in the sukah." The temporary quality of the sukah is a yearly reminder that real security lies in love of human beings and appreciation of God's universe, not in physical property or material things. A sukah is usually made of wood, with four walls and a roof open to the sky. The rabbis decreed that we should be able to see the stars at night, and so we place lattice work and fresh greens, branches, and other natural growth across the top. It is traditional to decorate the sukah by hanging fruits and vegetables of the season from the roof and walls.

The tangible nature of the sukah makes the holiday especially enjoyable for children. They love to help build and decorate it, to hold the *lulav* and the *etrog* and to say the blessings over them and the wine.

Simchat Torah

The day following the end of Sukot is called Simchat Torah (Rejoicing in the Torah). While there is no prescribed home observance, the synagogue ceremonies associated with the holiday are especially exciting for young children.

The holiday celebrates the finishing and the beginning again of the annual cycle of the reading of the Torah. Each Shabbat a portion of the Torah, the Five Books of Moses, is read. The portions follow one another in order and by Simchat Torah we have come to the end of the Book of Deuteronomy. That same night we read from the Book of Genesis as well, thus exemplifying in synagogue ritual the unending Jewish value of study. Great joy reigns in the synagogue as we remove all the Torah scrolls from the Ark, parade them around the sanctuary—seven times in traditional synagogues—then read from the end and the beginning of the Torah. In most synagogues, children follow the Torah processional, waving gaily colored flags and singing songs.

In most Reform congregations, Simchat Torah is also the time when children who have just entered the religious school receive a special blessing. This is the ceremony of Consecration. Often the new pupils recite the *Shema* then receive a small gift in honor of their first visit to the *bimah*.

Chanukah

Chanukah is the eight-day Jewish festival of freedom. It commemorates the victory of the Maccabees over the armies of Antiochus about 165 B.C.E. The word Chanukah means dedication, referring to the rededication of the Temple in Jerusalem which had been desecrated by the Syrian armies.

The menorah is the primary symbol of Chanukah. Each night we kindle the lights of the menorah, beginning with one candle and adding one each night until all eight lights are aglow. There is always one extra candle, called the *shamash*, or servant, which is used to light the others.

Long before Christian observance of Christmas entered the world of the Jews, Chanukah held excitement and joy for Jewish children. Games, plays, and special foods added other dimensions to this holiday of rededication. Interaction with the Christian world has added to the importance of Chanukah as a period of special light and gladness at the winter season.

For the modern Jew, Chanukah's meaning transcends candlelighting, gifts for children, and potato latkes. Of central significance is the recognition that an individual's religion must be an issue of personal choice, not the choice of the government under which the individual lives. The Maccabees of more than 2,000 years ago recognized this principle, which still eludes governments throughout the world today.

Thus, out of rejoicing over a significant victory in the history of the Jewish people, amid gift-giving and candlelighting, there emerges the resolve that every human being—in every part of the world—must be free to worship in the style which best suits that person's needs and way of life. And until every one lives in complete freedom to worship as he or she wishes, the message of Chanukah will not be fulfilled.

Tu Bishvat

A new year for the trees may seem strange, yet we have a minor holiday which is just that. It comes on the fifteenth day of the Hebrew month of Shevat, usually in February. Israelis go out to plant seedlings at this time. In North America, we plant trees around the synagogue or home, or donate money to plant trees that help reforest Israel. Money for that purpose is gathered in the familiar Jewish National Fund blue box. You may also send a sum directly to the JNF or the Union of American Hebrew Congregations for its forest projects in Israel. You will receive a certificate made out in your name, the name of your child, or anyone you may wish to honor. Planting a tree in Israel is a beautiful, living way of honoring or memorializing special people and events in your life.

Purim

Purim is a holiday based on the biblical Book of Esther. It is a tale filled with heroes and villains with whom people can easily identify: Mordechai, the hero of the day, who defies those bent on destroying the Jews; Esther, his cousin and adopted daughter, who risks her life for the people of Israel; Haman, the wicked prime

minister, who insulates and manipulates King Ahasuerus
and Vashti, the jilted queen.

The Jews were able to see their common lot in the
persecution and ultimate triumph of Mordechai and his
co-religionists in ancient Persia. The story of oppression
was all too familiar; the happy ending was one which
lent hope in the most perilous of times for the Jewish
people.

The synagogue ritual, centered on the reading of
Megillat Esther, has become one of the most popular in
Jewish folklore. Not only were the dearest hopes of the
Jewish people made manifest, but the natural hostility
against the many tyrants under whom Jews lived could
be healthily and safely expressed.

Thus, the normally serious mood of the synagogue is
given over to gaiety and delight. Noisemaking—with
greggers, pots, pans, foot stamping, booing—is allowed
when the name of the tyrant Haman is read from the
Megillah and cheers for heroes Mordechai and Esther
resound through every sanctuary.

Boys and girls dress up in costume and replay the
familiar story of the Scroll of Esther, especially the
contest which, the story relates, Esther won because of
her gentle beauty.

The gaiety is increased by parades, special three-
cornered pastry (hamantashen, called in Israel *oznei
haman),* and the sending of gifts of food (called *mish-
loach manot)* to friends and the needy.

But the essential message of Purim is never lost. Over
the centuries, Jews have suffered at the hands of cruel
oppressors, but none has yet been able to destroy the
people of Israel. Neither Czars, Hitlers, nor Soviet
commissars can conquer the indomitable spirit of the
Jewish people.

Pesach

For many Jews, Passover (or Pesach) is the central family holiday of the Jewish year. It celebrates both our freedom from Egyptian slavery and our establishment as a unique people. Orthodox Jews in the Diaspora observe the holiday for eight days while Reform Jews and the Jews of Israel observe the holiday for the biblically prescribed seven days.

More than any other holiday, Pesach is filled with symbolism, reminding us of slavery and freedom, the rebirth of nature, compassion for the needy, and hope for a radiant future. Families gather together on the first night of Pesach to share in the ritual of repeating the story of the Jewish people's exodus from Egyptian bondage to freedom in the Promised Land. The Seder, which combines almost every symbolic element of the Passover celebration, is conducted from the Haggadah, one of the most widely printed books in all of Jewish tradition.

There are synagogue services at Pesach, but the Seder is the focus of the holiday. Orthodox Jews prepare the home so that it will be entirely free of leaven, and they use a special set of Pesach dishes. Liberal Jews usually rid the home of leavened foods and may or may not have special Passover dishes, pots, and pans.

Seder nights are family nights. The Haggadah provides complete involvement for the children. In fact, they have an honored role. There are the Four Questions which are asked by the youngest child. In many families, they will be chanted first in Hebrew and then a younger child will read them in English.

There is the *afikoman*, a half of the central matzah, which is hidden at the beginning of the Seder. It is sought during the mealtime, and the child who discovers it receives a present before relinquishing it. The Seder itself is filled with stories and songs of freedom.

It's important for all children to participate. Even the smallest youngster should have a bit of wine and an opportunity to experience the Seder ritual.

Israel Independence Day

Yom Haatzmaut, Israel Independence Day, comes in April or May. It commemorates the establishment of the modern State of Israel on May 14th, 1948, which corresponded to the fifth day of the Hebrew month of Iyar.

Congregations now observe Yom Haatzmaut with special services of worship, which include Hebrew poetry, dance, and music created to capture the spirit of the Jewish state. In addition, some Reform synagogues hold Israel fairs, displaying Israeli-made products, and arts festivals highlighting the creative spirit of the Jewish people. Religious schools focus on the development of the Jewish state in story, song, and arts and crafts.

Shavuot

Shavuot is the third of the agriculturally based festivals of the Jewish year. Following seven weeks after Pesach, this harvest festival serves to remind the Jewish people of the closeness of our ancestors to the soil and their dependence on nature for their livelihood. Shavuot, Pesach, and Sukot are called "pilgrim festivals," for on these days Jews from all sections of Palestine brought thanksgiving offerings of their harvests to the Temple in Jerusalem.

Not only does Shavuot carry the message of nature, but a spiritual dimension was later added, that of the anniversary of the giving of the Torah on Mount Sinai. In a sense, it is the spiritual and cultural aspect of Shavuot that has helped the holiday to gain its present significance.

Each year at Shavuot, Liberal congregations mark the completion of one stage of the formal Jewish education of their students with the ceremony of Confirmation. This event symbolizes a renewed search for Jewish identity and a commitment to the Jewish value of life-long learning.

One way of celebrating Shavuot in your home is by lighting holiday candles, saying the *Kiddush,* and following the tradition of eating a dairy meal. Your home can be decorated with fruits and flowers for the holiday, and your child can assist in decorating. Shavuot itself can be a time of personal dedication to the constant search for new meanings in Judaism and Jewish ritual for you and your family.

8.

THE CEREMONIES
OF LIFE

Throughout its history, Judaism has generated life-cycle
ceremonies that are meaningful on many levels. From
birth to death, we mark the passage of time with religious rituals that help to sanctify life. As Judaism holds
that life is holy, it is understandable that the birth of a
child is one of our happiest and most meaningful occasions. There are formal ceremonies of baby-blessing,
circumcision, and baby-naming, as well as *pidyon haben*
when desired. These rituals involve not only the happy

family but the synagogue and community as well. In these ways, your child is welcomed into both your immediate family and the family of the Jewish people.

The Birth

When your baby is born, you may want to say a special prayer of thanks. Call your rabbi. He or she will want to share your happiness, to visit and join with you in reciting the blessing we say at all happy occasions:

Baruch Atah Adonai, Eloheinu Melech haolam, shehecheyanu, vikiyemanu vehigiyanu lazman hazeh.

"Blessed are You, O Lord, our God, Ruler of the universe, who has given us life, sustained us, and permitted us to reach this happy occasion."

Berit Milah—The Covenant of Circumcision

Circumcision of Jewish male babies on the eighth day of life as a sign of the *berit*, covenant, is almost four thousand years old. The Torah relates that Abraham was commanded to circumcise all males in his household. Since then, the operation and its accompanying ritual have been an accepted way of welcoming a baby boy into the Covenant of Israel. The usual Hebrew expression is *Berit Milah*, Covenant of Circumcision. It is often shortened to *berit*, emphasizing the spiritual bond between God, the infant, and his historical heritage. No other religious rite in Judaism is as old.

The Mohel

In ancient days, the *berit* ritual was performed by the father. As time passed, men gradually appeared who specialized in the operation as a religious duty. The *mohel,* circumciser, is a pious Jew who has studied the surgical procedure so as to be adept and knowledgeable. Today all professional *mohalim* must take courses in medicine and surgery and pass strict governmental examinations to obtain their special license.

Physicians have often commented that the eighth day seems to be an optimal time for the *berit.* The infant has managed to build up his physical resources, while the nervous system is relatively unformed. Consequently, the baby is usually back to his normal activities within minutes. More importantly, the medical world has come to recognize the value of circumcision in preventing exceedingly serious illness in later life.

Circumcision Today

Today just about every male child born in America, Jewish or not, is circumcised as a matter of course. The operation without any ritual has no Jewish significance. If a Jewish boy is not circumcised on the eighth day because of some exigency or health problem, the *Berit Milah* should take place when the emergency or health problem is past. If the boy is not circumcised for any reason, however, tradition still holds the boy a Jew, as long as the mother is Jewish.

It is customary for Orthodox parents to arrange for a *mohel* to perform the ritual in the home or in the synagogue if the *berit* takes place on Shabbat or a festival. Although it is a surgical operation, the ceremony is conducted by traditional Jews even on Yom Kippur or Shabbat in the synagogue after morning worship. The congregation is invited to remain and share in this joyous ceremony. There are some parts of the world where the *berit* is always held in the synagogue on any day of the week.

In many synagogues a special *Kisei Eliyahu*, Chair of Elijah, stands in a corner. The prophet Elijah is said to be invited to every *berit*, and he therefore is accorded a seat of honor.

Liberal Jewish Practice

Among Conservative and Reform Jews the *berit* is rarely performed in the synagogue. It usually takes place either in the home or in the hospital. Many hospitals have a special operating room which is used for *Berit Milah*. This enables parents to take their child home and then return for the ceremony on the eighth day.

All branches of Judaism discourage circumcision before the eighth day. As many hospitals routinely circumcise all male babies on the fourth or fifth day, you should advise your doctor of your intention to celebrate *Berit Milah*.

Preparing for the Ceremony

The eight days between birth and *Berit Milah* are counted from the day of birth. Therefore, a child born on a Monday is circumcised the next Monday.

A lovely traditional custom which you may wish to include as part of your personal observance is a "feast" on the Shabbat Eve preceding the day of the *berit*.

Friends and family are present at this time of joy, and fruits and beverages are served.

On the day of the ceremony, family and friends assemble at the home, hospital, or synagogue. It is customary to have a *minyan*, quorum of ten Jews, present. In Reform Judaism, both men and women are counted as members of the *minyan* and are full participants in the ritual. Traditionally, a chair is set aside for the prophet Elijah. The head of the house or the *mohel* says in Hebrew: "This is the Chair of Elijah the prophet; may his remembrance be for good." The child is brought in and rested on the chair for a moment as though placed on Elijah's lap.

All those present remain standing for the entire ceremony, except the *sandak*, the godfather, who holds the baby for the operation.

Godparents

There are two or even three godparents at a *berit:* the *sandak*, holding the child during the ceremony, a position of great honor, and the *kvatter* and *kvatterine*, the godfather and godmother. The *sandak* and *kvatter* may be the same person. The *sandak's* role in holding the baby has been eased in recent years as there is now a shaped form into which the infant is strapped to keep him from moving too much. Most *mohalim* and surgeons use it.

The godparents have future duties, to be responsible with the parents for the religious training of the child. As such, they should be Jews who are close to the family and who take their Judaism seriously.

The Ceremony

The *mohel* begins by passing the infant from Elijah's chair to the godfather and the godmother. They each hold the baby for a moment as a sign of assuming partial responsibility for the spiritual rearing of their godson. The father then takes the child and hands him to the *sandak*, and the baby is made ready for the ceremony and the operation.

If two infants are to be circumcised at the same time, twin brothers, for example, each has a full ceremony, so that each may have all the blessings recited for his sake. A meal in honor of the observance of a *mitzvah* usually follows. The complete Reform ceremony for *Berit Milah* may be found in *Gates of the House* (CCAR, 1976).

A New Ceremony for Girls

In recent years, many Liberal Jews have developed special ceremonies for welcoming newborn daughters into Judaism. Like *Berit Milah*, it takes place on the eighth day following birth.

One of the loveliest such ceremonies, called *The Covenant of Life*, may be found in *Gates of the House*. Both the mother and father recite special blessings, the *Kiddush* is chanted, and the priestly benediction is pronounced over the infant. It is a fitting and meaningful way to express joy and thanks for the gift of a new daughter.

9.

A NAME BLESSED
IN ISRAEL

The Names

It is fitting to give Jewish children Jewish
names. They should also receive Hebrew names which
may be identical with the English ones. Names that
signify other religions, such as Christopher, Matthew,
Luke, John, and Noel, or Christine, Mary, Madeline,
Dolores, and the like are usually avoided. Biblical
names like Daniel, David, Joel, and Eli, or Ruth, Rachel,

56

Deborah, and Naomi are beautiful and fitting. So are many Israeli names: Carmi, Uri, Aliza, Ora, Shoshana, and many others. Your child's Hebrew name may be the same as the English or may be related by sound or translation. The name is expressed as X *ben* Y, X the son of Y; or X *bat* Y, X the daughter of Y, Y being the father's Hebrew name. Many rabbis will say that the name is *ben* or *bat* Y and Z, Z being the mother's Hebrew name. This is not as new an idea as it may sound, as many rabbinic leaders of the past were known as the sons of their mothers—as, for instance, the renowned Levi Yitzhak who was always *ben* Sarah. Your child's Hebrew name will be used at Bar or Bat Mitzvah time, at his or her marriage—and many synagogues call up readers to the Torah by the Hebrew names. If there is any difficulty in finding a Hebrew name, your rabbi can readily help you find a pleasing one.

After Whom

It has long been an Ashkenazic Jewish tradition to name a child after a deceased relative. It is a meaningful tradition that brings comfort to many. A boy may be named for a grandmother, a girl for a great uncle. Many Hebrew names have masculine or feminine equivalents, but, where this is not so, the rabbi will help find a proper one.

Central European (Ashkenazic) Jews never name a child for a living relation, whereas Iberian (Sephardic) and Oriental Jews do. The Ashkenazic ban was based on the superstitious fear that the angel of death might confuse the two with the same name. Most Jews today still do not name for the living, not because of superstition, but, rather, because of concern for the self-identity of the individual.

Adopted Children

Adopted children, even those of non-Jewish birth, are considered Jews from the moment of their *Berit Milah* or baby-naming. Boys should be circumcised on the eighth day or as soon after as possible. Both boys and girls are given Hebrew names as the child of their adoptive father and mother. If you adopt older children, you may wish to have a formal conversion ceremony when the child understands what is involved. In either case, the children should be raised and educated as full, participating members of the Jewish religion.

The Traditional Way

After the birth of a child, a traditional father attends the first service in the synagogue at which the Torah is read (Shabbat, Monday, Thursday, festival, or high holy day). He informs the rabbi or *shamash* (sexton) of the birth and is called to the reading of the Torah. After his *aliyah* (wherein he chants the Torah *berachot* before and after a portion of the reading), the rabbi or *shamash* chants a *misheberach*, a special blessing for the mother and child. As the *berit* includes the naming ceremony for boys, only girls are blessed and named during this special *berachah*. It reads:

"May He who blessed our fathers, Abraham, Isaac, and Jacob,* bless _____, the son of _____, and his

*In some synagogues today, the following words are added: "And our mothers, Sarah, Rebekah, Rachel, and Leah."

daughter born unto him. May her name be known in Israel as _____, the daughter of _____. O guard and protect her father and mother, and may they live to rear her in fear of God, for the nuptial canopy, and for a life of good deeds, and let us say, Amen."

The Liberal Naming

If the naming is in a Liberal synagogue, it usually takes place as part of the service on a Shabbat evening or morning, with the entire family present. The appropriate day is the first Shabbat the mother is able to attend.

Each congregation orders the baby-naming as it thinks appropriate. It is a brief but beautiful ceremony. In Reform synagogues, the baby is given both a secular and a Hebrew name.

In some congregations, the baby-naming is a family affair. The infant is brought to the synagogue at a non-service time. The father or mother holds the child during the ceremony which is conducted in the sanctuary or chapel. The brief ceremony consists of a prayer of thanksgiving, the naming—including both English and Hebrew names—and the blessing of the baby by the rabbi. Though *Berit Milah* technically names a Jewish boy, Reform parents usually have both boys and girls named in the temple.

Pidyon Haben

There is an ancient Jewish custom involving first-born male children that has all but disappeared in Reform Judaism. The ritual is called *Pidyon Haben*. The

Hebrew words *pidyon haben* mean "redemption of the
son," the first-born male child of the mother.

Why would a first-born son need to be redeemed? The
Torah tells us that the *petter rechem*, the male offspring
that "opens the womb," belongs to God (Exodus 13:2
and Numbers 8:16). In ancient times, the child was
turned over to the priest for a life of religious service in
the Temple in Jerusalem. (See the Story of Hannah and
Samuel in I Samuel, chapters 1-2.)

Over the centuries, the custom arose that a father
would redeem his son from the priest for five silver
pieces in lieu of Temple service. After the destruction of
the Temple, the ritual lived on in an exchange between a
father and a *Kohen*—any Jew who could trace his ances-
try to the temple priests. If either father or mother is a
descendant of the *Kohanim* (Aaronic priests) or *Leviim*
(Levite) families, the *Pidyon Haben* is unnecessary.

The contemporary traditional ceremony is brief. The
father presents his son to the *Kohen*, then places five
silver coins before him. The *Kohen* asks which he pre-
fers, to keep the child by redeeming him with silver
coins or to give him to the *Kohen*. The father responds
that he would rather redeem his baby with the coins and
receives the baby back. The father then recites two
blessings:

*Baruch Atah Adonai, Eloheinu Melech haolam,
asher kideshanu bemitzvotav vetzivanu al pidyon haben.*

"Blessed are You, O Lord our God, Ruler of the
universe, who hallowed us in His mitzvot and commanded us concerning the redemption of the first-born
son."

*Baruch Atah Adonai, Eloheinu Melech haolam,
shehecheyanu, vekiyemanu, vehigiyanu lazman hazeh.*

"Blessed are You, O Lord our God, Ruler of the universe, who has given us life, sustained us, and permitted us to reach this happy occasion."

The *Kohen* takes the coins and holds them over the head of the son. He says, "This for that, this in commutation for that, this in remission for that. May this child enter into life, to the Torah, and to the fear of Heaven. May it be God's will that even as he has been admitted into redemption, so may he enter into the Torah, the nuptial canopy, and to good deeds. Amen."

The *Kohen*, the father, and all assembled then join in a party in celebration of the performance of a *mitzvah*. It is traditional to contribute the coins or a larger sum to a Jewish charity.

The entire traditional ceremony can be found in every large Orthodox *siddur*, prayer book. It is usually held on the thirty-first day after the baby's birth. Should this day fall on a Shabbat, festival, or high holy day, it is postponed until the next day.

Reform Judaism has never assigned a major priority to *Pidyon Haben* as its rationale is somewhat anachronistic in modern times. There are, however, some Reform families who continue to value and practice the ritual, an expression of the freedom inherent in Reform.

If you would like to have a *Pidyon Haben* ceremony, consult your rabbi.

10.

GRANDPARENTS

Special People

Grandparents usually have the best of all the wonderful joy of their grandchildren with little of the daily care and chores. They also have a special role in their grandchildren's religious education. They represent tradition, the history, the unity of the family. Through them a sense of continuity and achievement is manifest. Grandparents give children a feeling of rootedness, of belonging, of humanity and its values—and of time passing.

The rabbis spoke in praise of grandparents, and the Torah tells us to rise before those who have reached a goodly age. They are considered repositories of knowledge and wisdom.

The benefits of having and seeing grandparents are numerous. It is wonderful for children to have grandparents who live near, visit, and are visited often. Distant grandparents have an honored place, but their beneficial role is in accord with the time they can spend with their grandchildren.

The youngster with grandparents nearby has another real home. It is a home to share, and one in which to find sympathy, patience, and love. Horizons are widened. Grandparents often have more time to share new experiences and discoveries. They can help give children a sense of recognition and importance. This is obviously so if both parents work or if there are many siblings. A child who feels overlooked may find attention and support at his or her "second home."

Jewish Roots

But even when children have no risk of being overlooked, the grandparents' role is important. They listen, speak of their own lives, and relate the story of their own childhoods, which fascinates children and makes them feel part of the past.

Few grandparents today have roots in the shtetl, the small Eastern European town. Yet those who had an intense Jewish upbringing can impart a sense of community and religion that our modern world often lacks.

Grandparents offer a special gift, themselves and their own sense of religion. The child will grasp the role of religion in the lives of the grandparents from their home, their daily habits, from their responses as well as from direct teachings. Their home, with its gathered Jewish objects, books, and art works, makes an immediate impression. Grandparents can help you teach Judaism to your children: telling biblical stories or legends, singing a favorite Jewish song, taking children to the synagogue on a Shabbat or holiday, or helping to observe Shabbat or a holiday at home. Grandparents can foster a sense of religious commitment and love of Judaism. Their love for their children and grandchildren—and their personal example—bring a precious addition to a child's life.

11.

DEATH AND THE AFTERLIFE

The Response to Death

It would be so convenient if we never had to
teach our children anything at all about death and the
afterlife. But the world impinges. A grandparent may
die, or a relative, or the grandparent of a neighbor or
friend. A dog or cat dies, or your youngster sees a dead
bird. The face is saddened and questions come. What do
we do? What do we say?

65

Should you just try to divert the child? No, you must answer to some degree. Full answers may not be required, but partial answers, honest answers, are needed. A response about heaven is too easy. It is a lesson that would have to be unlearned at some future time. It would cause anger and anxiety after your child grows to discover that you do not believe in such a heaven where grandparents and dogs and cats sit about waiting for us to join them.

Death Is a Stranger

The question of life and death is unreal to most children. Life overshadows death. "Pow, pow, you're dead!" children shout. But the victim always rises to resume play. Children watch characters die on TV. Then they reappear in the same or another show. Children hear of actors' deaths, yet there they are again next week in another movie.

A child feels immortal. Oliver Wendell Holmes II spoke of this feeling when he was young and felt sure that if he lost a finger that he would grow one again as a salamander grows a new tail.

So death ordinarily does not threaten a child. Hearing of the death of a relative has little effect, for it does not threaten the child's immediate world and family. It is something that happens to others. The death of a pet can affect the child more than the passing of a real but distant uncle. A dog rushes into the path of a car; the child is confronted with extinction. A pet's death can leave a child inconsolable for a while. How much more so will a child be affected by the death of a near and dear relative, a person who has loved the child and been loved in return. This can be a shattering experience that opens questions that barely existed before.

The Deprivation

The child feels threatened as well as deprived and sorrowful. Suddenly his or her parents become vulnerable, and so do all siblings, uncles, aunts, friends. The idea may occur that the young are also vulnerable and that everyone, including the child, must eventually die. Age is no guarantee. The idea of physical immortality may disappear and mortality, with all its fears, takes its place. Coupled with mortality may be fears and suppositions beyond reality.

Death means that the beings who provide security and love may be taken away. The shock of such discovery may be great and lasting. The immediate remedy is abundant love and concern. Parents must not brush off the shock as something that will pass of itself, though it may. Some children will not show concern overtly. They may hide their emotion when they see that it distresses their parents, yet continue to grieve silently. This may be manifested in failure to eat, bad dreams, peevishness, or periods of unaccustomed quiet. Some children seem to be able to thrust death aside, refusing to allow it to bother them. There are others who are too immature to grasp what is involved. It is often difficult to establish whether children are sloughing it off easily or are hiding their vital concern and worrying fear. Each child's parents must try to decide after their child has been confronted with death. If there is a chance that the concern of the child is real, the parents must try to respond.

Parents' Response

First, by far, is tender loving care, the "TLC" that people often speak about. It should always be part of your child's world, but for sometime afterwards it should be increased with physical hugs, kisses, warmth, and tenderness. There must be some discussion and explanation. Each child's parents must decide how much. This is one instance where a bit too little may be better than just a bit too much. Gauge your child. If there seems to be interest and understanding, continue a bit. Do not continue if you detect uneasiness, boredom, or a desire on your child's part to change the subject.

If your child asks, you must answer. If there seem to be signs of distress, you try to bring up the subject. The classical Reform Jewish presentation includes the eternity of God, for some children may even worry that God might die and the world with Him. God cares for all life, and He has given to each person a living soul. The human soul is a portion of God lent to each of us, and eventually we all must return it to God. The soul will live with God.

The child may protest and even accuse God of taking to Himself something dear. Our answer is that God takes back to Himself that which dies, but God does not kill. It is not God who causes an aged person to die, but the gradual ending of a life that has been full and long. It is not God who causes an accident, but the careless use or mechanical malfunctions of cars and planes. It is not God who causes disease, but the imperfection of nature.

Our Judaism says that it is according to God's plan for humanity that we develop our scientific knowledge and use it to save lives. But whenever someone dies, for whatever reason, Judaism teaches that God takes the soul back to Himself.

Do not ever offer the idea of hell to your child. Even heaven must be soft-pedaled, for *Gan Eden*, the Garden of Eden, the usual Hebrew designation of paradise, is a beautiful idea but one the rabbis did not stress. It is much too easy to offer heaven, the heaven of wings and halos, of families reunited and all accounts nicely balanced. Do so, if you believe it yourself—and many Jews do. But not otherwise. The idea of the dead living on with God is the more usual Liberal Jewish teaching. The best single book on this subject is *Talking about Death: A Dialogue between Parent and Child,* by Rabbi Earl Grollman (Beacon). You should have a copy in your home library.

Some Jews are under the impression that Judaism does not believe in a spiritual afterlife. There is no question that traditional Judaism *does* articulate a belief in the soul's living on with God:

"O my God, the soul which Thou gavest me is pure; Thou didst create it, Thou didst form it, Thou didst breathe it into me. Thou preservest it within me, and Thou will take it from me but will restore unto me thereafter. . ." (Hertz, *The Authorized Daily Prayer Book,* p. 19).

The Jewish philosopher, Maimonides, in his Thirteen Principles of Faith, goes much further:

"I believe with perfect faith that there will be a revival of the dead at the time when it shall please the Creator. . . ." Orthodoxy affirms bodily resurrection: "Blessed art Thou, O Lord, who quickenest the dead."

Our Reform movement affirms the eternity of the soul: ". . . Who implanted within us eternal life." This mirrors the thought: "The dust returns to the dust as it was, but the spirit returns to God who gave it" (Ecclesiastes 12:7).

Whether you accept an Orthodox or more liberal Jewish interpretation, Judaism teaches that the spirit does not cease with death. Death is cessation of life as we know it, but the dead do not live on only in our memories or in the deeds of goodness they performed. They also live in spirit with God, as well as through memory and deed.

Very gradually, a child will understand that there is no final separation between the living and the dead. Through memory, through love, we remain together. We live to honor their memory, and they live on with God.

Your Faith

The child's awareness of our belief in the soul and its immortality is attained through your words and attitudes.

Responding may be difficult for you when faced by a worried child. This may be especially true on the death of a grandparent, when you are torn by personal grief. It may be difficult to respond with care and patience at such a time. But if out of your own faith and love you can comfort a worried and grieving child, you will have done so very much.

A friendly and assuring word is in order here. Many parents have discovered that, in the midst of their own grief, the need to minister to the perplexed and equally grieving child acts as a source of strength and comfort to themselves. The presence of children and their obvious love present an object lesson in our own role. We are in touch with the cycle of eternity, and this gives us strength and comfort.

The recital of the *Kaddish* prayer for the deceased will

also help. Your children will not understand the affirmation of life this prayer affords. They will, however, see
the strength that the synagogue, prayer service, and the
presence of the congregation provide. That the rabbi
will probably lead the recitation of the *Kaddish* is also a
strengthening agent. Not that the *Kaddish* must be
recited by a rabbi. It can be recited by any Jew. But the
rabbi is the representative of tradition. To children, the
rabbi is often a symbol of God, and his or her presence
can be comforting to children and parents alike.

A Funeral

Most psychologists agree that children as well
as adults need to experience the finality of a loved one's
death in order to successfully move through the stages of
grief and mourning. Very small children should not be
brought to a funeral, as the experience may be filled with
fear and anxiety.

As in moments of family joy, it is important for children to feel that they are an integral and important part
of the family when tragedy strikes as well. Whenever
children reach an age where they wish to attend the
funeral and participate with the family, they should be
encouraged to do so.

It is often helpful, when a child is about to attend his
or her first funeral, for a parent to explain exactly what
will happen, so the child will know what to expect. The
fantasies and fears of children are often much more
gruesome and unpleasant than the reality of the funeral.

12.

HELL AND THE DEVIL

There was a time when a discussion of hell and the devil would not have appeared in a book for Jewish parents. But times have changed. Movies like *The Exorcist,* as well as numerous television shows and dramas, have brought these topics into everyday conversation. Children cannot help but hear the terminology and begin to ask questions—questions which you should be prepared to answer.

The Devil or Satan

The word "devil" occurs in the Torah only twice, both times as a warning not to sacrifice to "the devils of the heathen." Satan does occur by name in Job and fleetingly in Zechariah, Chronicles, and one time in Psalms. Satan plays a decidedly minor role in classical Jewish theology and none whatsoever in modern Jewish thought. He is not a fallen angel nor does he have a realm of his own. He is not God's antagonist, for our God is one, with none like Him. In the literary world portrayed by Isaac Bashevis Singer, there is a Satan who has hordes of imps and demons. They try to catch people committing sins so that they will have companions in their misery. This makes for strong fiction, but it is born of superstition and folklore.

According to the Midrash, when God wished to create the world He counselled with the angels of His court as to whether He should also create humankind. One angel was vehemently against man's creation for, he averred, man would sin. But God decided to create people for the sake of the good deeds they would do. The protesting angel was assigned the task of informing God when man sins. Hence, he is called Satan, the adversary—man's adversary, not God's.

In short, then, while Satan plays a poetic or symbolic role in some Jewish writings, the devil idea is not a part of modern Jewish thought or teaching.

Gehenna, Hell, Inferno

Nor does modern Jewish thought speak of a hell. The idea of an eternal hell, a place of everlasting torment, as in Dante's *Divine Comedy*, is completely foreign to our understanding.

In classical Judaism, the place of cleansing in the afterlife is called *gehenna*. *Gei Hinom* is a valley south of Jerusalem. A man named Hinom owned the valley in ancient days. More than two and a half thousand years ago, the valley was the scene of idol worship. After the reforms of King Josiah the valley was deliberately turned into a garbage dump. The odors, the smoke, and flames of the burning garbage and the memory of ancient blasphemy helped produce the idea that whatever hell existed would be similar. Today it is a peaceful place, far removed from history or legend.

There is no everlasting *gehenna* or hell in normative Judaism. Classical Judaism holds that the cleansing of the soul never takes longer than one year, after which the soul returns to God. At worst, *gehenna* is a purgatory. Only chasidic Jews, today, speak of an afterlife that entails punishment or cleansing of more than a year's duration.

The Kaddish

The *Kaddish*, which is recited in memory of the dead, is a perfect example of the Jewish response to death and its refusal to worry about punishment in the afterlife. The *Kaddish* prayer as recited in our synagogues, both traditional and liberal, contains no mention of the dead. Instead, it is an affirmation of life, of our belief in God, and our need to work for a world of peace.

The *El Malei Rachamim*, the special prayer recited at funerals and at *Yizkor* (memorial) services, does speak directly to the memory of the dead. It asks God to take our beloved under the "shelter of His wings," a poetic image of great beauty, and of "binding their souls in the bond of eternal life." Both prayers are entirely positive and speak of affirming our belief in God's goodness.

The constant Jewish understanding has been that of Antigonos of Socho, quoted in the *Sayings of the Fathers:* "Be not like servants who serve their master in hope of reward" (Avot 1:3). He closed: "And let the fear of heaven be upon you." The fear of heaven, but not the fear of hell. We revere God and honor His teachings. Out of this sense of reverence comes our recognition of our role as Jews. Judaism is positive and God is compassionate. When we teach our children, the emphasis should always be on the joy of doing well, of a world bettered by our actions.

Conclusion:

The Importance of Silent Teaching

The Emotional Atmosphere

There is an old midrash that tells of two angels who go about the world every Shabbat Eve and peer through the windows of each Jewish home. If the table is set, Shabbat candles lit, and all is peace, the good angel says: "May this home be like this next week!" and the bad angel must respond: "Amen." If, however, there is no Shabbat preparation and strife prevails, then the bad angel says: "May this home be like this next week!" and the good angel must say: "Amen."

The atmosphere of a home is characterized by the presence or absence of love, understanding, and religious spirit. Their presence fulfills the prime duty of parenthood by answering the child's vital needs of security in physical, psychological, and emotional terms.

During the first months, when the infant depends totally on the parents, patterns of security and interrelationship are established. If parents cannot provide these necessities, insecurity results. The baby learns fear instead of confidence and the sense of being loved.

As your children mature, they will develop a growing awareness of the world. People will become individuals and the baby will learn that he or she is a person. If you demonstrate love, your children will learn to accept love as a natural part of life and to respond with their own

76

affection and trust. Freud believed that those who left Judaism almost always had a difficult childhood in a tense home atmosphere. Unless children learned to love and be loved, Freud affirmed, they would find it hard to love God and Judaism as well.

The rabbis said that parents are God's surrogates on earth. In our tradition, God is loving and compassionate. We must try to exemplify this whenever we deal with our children.

Acceptance

A baby needs a sense of belonging. When children are part of a family, they will be able to develop into people who respect their own beings and can love in return.

We sometimes forget that attitudes and non-verbal responses can be either supportive or as cruel as harsh spoken words. The emotional climate of your family is crucial. A child has not yet been able to build defenses. He or she can only sense, feel, and react. When children sense anger and rejection, their pride and sensibility suffer. Conversely, in experiencing family unity, concern, and love, plus the aura of a positive Jewish home, they are reinforced in building their own personality and spirit.

The Very Young Child

The first months of a baby's life are wordless, but babies are surrounded by communication, by signs of love, of joy, even of reproof. This is the initial vocabu-

lary received by their receptive minds and sensibil-
ities. Gradually, children move from the passive to the
active as they learn their own responses to the parents'
words.

So love and the sense of belonging are communicated
to the infant in non-verbal language. Tone of speech and
gesture are comprehended. The baby assimilates the
good and the bad, and your home atmosphere is the
determining factor.

Basic Trust

Signs of love indicate acceptance to babies'
wakening minds and establish the set of their relationship to the universe. You extend your arms to pick up
your baby. It is brought into warm contact with your
body. It is nestled and feels loved. Siblings and relatives
vie to express their own delight. Through these natural
expressions a child receives its sense of belonging.

This is what Erik H. Erikson calls "basic trust" and
"wholeness." Basic trust is the feeling that flows between infants and their parents. It is a "general sense of
warmth and mutuality, an actual sense of the reality of
'good' powers, outside and within oneself." Basic trust is
the groundwork of mature identity. It enables the de-
veloping person "to combine a sense of being 'all right,'
of being oneself and of becoming what other people trust
one will become." The quality of trust is developed by
the initial relationship between parents and infant. It
becomes a sense of trust in life and can lead to spiritual
trust as well.

"Wholeness," as Erikson presents it, is a very Jewish
quality and may well be a heritage of his own Jewish

religious training in pre-Hitler Germany. Wholeness calls on children to develop as a whole, accepting their parents and past, their belonging, their impulses and needs. This capacity to synthesize the complex diverse and disparate strands of our being finds its roots in the relationship of trust between parents and infant, within the home as the center of family warmth. It is interesting to note that "wholeness" in Hebrew is *shalem* and immediately related to *shalom,* peace.

God and the Father and the Mother

The child's response to the idea of God is born of this familial love and mutual trust. The child recognizes that it is part of God's love and God's world. The parents ask God's blessing on their children at bedtime, until they are old enough to pray for themselves. The child sees, listens, and soon participates in the saying of the *Motzi,* the grace over bread, that begins each meal. There is a turning to Someone greater than ourselves in gratitude for food, family, and existence. The child sees the preparation for Shabbat and holidays, the candles lit, the wine glass lifted, the blessings, the joy of Shabbat or holiday.

The moment before the parent turns from the child at bedtime can establish a sense of peace at going to sleep or can contribute to a sense of deprivation. If parents show their love and faith in God as part of saying good night, children will build within themselves a sense of trust in God.

The words of prayer need not be formal. Later the child will learn the *Shema,* but at first, even in the first few weeks of life, a parent should speak a few words of blessing and gratitude. Perhaps, "O God, we thank You for our child. Keep us in Your love," or something similar. The precise words are unimportant. It is the reaching out in prayer, the sense of commitment. On-coming sleep has been greeted as a welcome friend.

The Challenge to Be

In the course of the preceding chapters, we have examined a host of possible ways in which you might begin to build a Jewish home. In every instance, we have tried to indicate concrete examples of that which you can *do* to achieve that important goal.

But, when all is said and done, we must not only *do*. We must *be*. Perhaps the poet Emerson captured our sentiments best when he said: "I cannot hear what you *say*, for what you *are* is thundering in my ears." Ulti-mately, our children must know that our Judaism is a valued part of our own lives. For if we only pay lip service to a faith and a way of life that is not our own, they will see and understand. Silent teaching, then, is as important, if not more so, than any formal lesson. And it is with that thought that we conclude.

Love, acceptance, warmth, and the model of our own lives are the means through which our children will come to know their world and their Judaism. May we be sensitive to that great responsibility and successful in maximizing our potential and that of our children as well.

Your Home Library
—A Starter List

A Jewish home without a Jewish library is a contradiction. You can *never* have too many Jewish books.

Your library will grow from year to year, and, with it, your family's knowledge and appreciation of our rich Jewish heritage. The following is a list of books with which you might begin.

Encyclopedias

Encyclopaedia Judaica. Jerusalem: Keter, 1972, 16 volumes.

The New Jewish Encyclopedia. David Bridger, ed. New York: Behrman House. A good one-volume reference.

The Standard Jewish Encyclopedia. Cecil Roth, ed. Garden City: Doubleday and Co. The largest one-vollume reference work.

Histories

Dimont, Max. *Jews, God and History.* New York: Simon and Schuster, 1962.

Grayzel, Solomon. *A History of the Jews.* Philadelphia: JPS, 1953.

Roth, Cecil. *A History of the Jews.* New York: Schocken, 1966.

Sachar, Abram Leon. *A History of the Jews.* New York: Knopf, 1965.

81

Scripture

Genesis Torah Commentary. Gunther Plaut, ed. New York: UAHC, 1974.

Pentateuch and Haftorahs. Joseph H. Hertz, ed. London: Soncino, various dates.

The Torah. Philadelphia: JPS., 1962. Plus various other books of the Bible.

The Holy Scriptures. Philadelphia: JPS., 1917.

Prayer Books

Gates of Prayer, Shaarei Tefillah. New York: CCAR, 1975. The Reform Shabbat and daily prayer book.

Gates of Repentance, Shaarei Teshuvah. New York: CCAR, 1978. The Reform High Holy Day prayer book.

Jewish Living

Bial, Morrison David. *Liberal Judaism at Home,* New York: UAHC, 1971. Background and explanation of Reform Jewish practices.

_____. *The Questions You Asked,* New York: Behrman House, 1972. Questions and answers on liberal Jewish thought.

Freeman, Grace, and Sugarman, Joan. *Inside the Synagogue.* New York: UAHC, 1963. Lovely illustrations, the synagogue affectionately presented.

Gates of the House. New York: CCAR, 1976. A guide to Reform Jewish home observance.

Schauss, Hayyim. *The Jewish Festivals.* New York: Schocken. 1962.

———. *The Lifetime of a Jew.* New York: UAHC. 1950.
A Shabbat Manual. New York: CCAR, 1972. A Reform
   presentation; all you need for home observance.
Syme, Daniel B. *The Jewish Home.* New York: UAHC,
   several pamphlets, various dates. Concise presenta-
   tions of many aspects of Jewish home observances.